Equanimity - an inspiration

Deepti Belliappa Ganapathy

Presentation by *BookLeaf Publishing*

Web: www.bookleafpub.com

E-mail: info@bookleafpub.com

ISBN: 9789363314405

First edition 2024

To everyone who believes in the magic of life!

Live. Love. Laugh

ACKNOWLEDGEMENT

With love and thanks to my parents, brother, husband and children for their enduring patience and being a part of my life journey as I continue to grow as a person.

I am grateful to my professional community who has given me the confidence of seeing inspiration in everything around us and giving me my wings to ink from my heart. .

I am deeply grateful to my family and friends who have stood by me with their unwavering support and honest guidance always.

I acknowledge the support of the team at Bookleaf Publishing who has worked with me tirelessly to bring this book to its fruition.

PREFACE

The Paradox of Our Age—perhaps crafted by multiple authors but stuck with me when it was shared by the Dalai Lama. Every word is a reality and I see the truth around me. This inspiration has stayed with me to build this book every step of the way, hope you see it too…

The paradox of our age
We have bigger houses but smaller families;
more conveniences, but less time;
We have more degrees, but less sense;
more knowledge, but less judgment;
more experts, but more problems;
more medicines, but less healthiness;
We've been all the way to the moon and back,
but have trouble crossing the street to meet the new neighbour.
We built more computers to hold more information
to produce more copies than ever, but have less communication;
We have become long on quantity, but short on quality.
These are times of fast foods but slow digestion;
Tall man but short character;
Steep profits but shallow relationships.
It's a time when there is much in the window,
but nothing in the room.

The great escape

The daily grind, the many meltdowns are there,
Travel often feels like the best care.
A trip with friends or that dreamy solo trip,
Where everything is in my own grip.

But the plan with the family needs proper care,
Little details are a family affair.
Options are many, finalise one place at the end,
Plan the itinerary and book to the last second.

As the days near, packing, lists, documents in tow,
Wardrobe drama for the perfect photo show.
Mixed emotions are there for sure,
But awaiting that journey here.

The airport chaos has its own charm,
Staying cool, pulling our trolley with the right arm.
The quick bite and the brewing coffee here,
Sets the mood for much cheer.

The turbulent flights or the delayed pick,
Many confusions but staying calm is the trick.
The waves sound, the sights of the mountain green,
The heart flutters like nothing it has seen.

The blue of the sea, the history that grips,
The mind is reminded of some iconic trips.
As we blend with the vibe of the locals there,
The hospitality and warmth is gripping to share.

Many cultures, lessons to be learned in time,
Every experience here is truly sublime.
We return home with a heavy heart,
Leaving behind an almost new start.

But something does stay with us for sure,
Newer hopes, dreams, ideas and values here.
As we hope to ape some learning from our trip,
It's time to get back to the normal grip.

Reality at home, laundry piled, grocery to check,
Billed now, time to pay, be quick.
Smitten by the travel bug, let's open Google soon,
The next destination in plan, it's time to swoon!

Nostalgia – Looking back, smiling ahead

Floppies, VCR, pager are words of the past,
No one knows when they saw it last.
The endless winding of the cassette with a pencil,
Save the tape and hear the last musical.

Photos had to be taken with care,
The limited film reel was an irreversible scare.
The dial-up internet and struggling connections,
ICQ chats were unnamed equations.

Music played on the Walkman in tow,
Doordarshan, Ramayan was a family show.
The TV needed the antenna swayed by the wind,
The melody of ads remained pinned.

Washing powder Nirma or Liril soap for sure,
The Onida devil or the dancing Dairy Milk girl's
cheer.
Rasna, Gold Spot, Thums Up, Roohavza to sip,
Or be cool by 'being you' in the Fido Dido clip.

The scent of Old Spice & Brylcreem in your dad's kit,
Polish and Blanco the Bata shoes for a perfect fit.
The iconic Ambassador, blue for us stood tall,
The rolling windows, a memory for all!

The mess of filling out fountain pens in time,
The priced Reynolds was worth every dime.
Camlin pencils and Geometry box in every bag,
With books bound in brown and a label to tag.

Teachers taught and we had to hear them say,
No Google could save us after that day.
Encyclopedia was our project guide,
With newspaper cuttings on the side.

Phantom Sweet Cigarettes or a Mango Bite,
Poppins, Hajmola had its might.
Cat's Cradle, Hopscotch, had endless fun,
The mystery of FLAMES was number one.

Paper boats or planes and chits were passed,
The best form of messaging that could be asked.
The postman had a big role to play,
Letters, postcards, stamps made our day.

Money denominations saw Re 1 and 2,
We even counted paisa 5, 10 and 20 too.
Diwali crackers with the Bijli and gun,
The crawly snake that appeared was quirky fun.

Shikari Shambu and Suppandi had us gripped,
Tinkle and Amar Chitra Katha had us flipped.
An oddly muscular He-Man seemed to charm,
Barbie definitely never lost its glam.

Life in the 80's to 90's will know this dwindling past,
Reliving a memory so strong it's bound to last.
Captured this memory lane as it will fade for sure,
This timeline will always be remembered with cheer.

Breaking the shackles

Life from 1 to 99 has plenty to see,
A perplexing constraint, and a struggle to compete!
If you are born with a slightly darker skin tone,
Relatives are quick to comment in that zone.

The student grapples with grades that matter,
It's time to impress the school or society's chatter.
Selections and future depend on an exceptional score,
What happens to those who didn't make it to the fore.

Comparisons are many and often one is told,
Learn from another, forgetting their unique mould,
We get tangled in our own stereotypes for sure,
Overlooking the unexpected excel beyond one here.

The construction worker will do his might to earn,
Educating his child for a better career is his concern.
Many personalities thrive some loud and not always
right,
The fear of judgment, the unspoken do not fight.

Some push boundaries with books and work to ace,
Or get tangled in primitive minds resisting the pace.
Career choices are many for sure,
But limited minds can only see value in a few here.

Praises for Doctors, Engineers and Lawyers now,
The radical professions yearn for glory in their show.
Marriage for most, balance is the name,
Often women take the back seat in this game.

Many women win both worlds with grace,
Shield unforgiving judgments as mothers in this race.
Pressure on men to feed the home with their might,
It's an unfortunate partial view; not an equal fight.

Parents today have split their roles fair,
Applauds only to the dad while mum does her share.
Marriages can be fragile and may not see the end,
But individuals are often pushed to not let it bend.

The mind is burdened with pressure, yet we smile,
Even though one may be breaking at every mile.
Yearning for a liberated society that we read,
It's a tall task that we urge with speed.

Mental well-being is a looming conundrum for sure,
Ask for help and get your cure.
The society often forgets the silent soul,
Find your balance and believe in your goal.

Time Out

Exhilarating thrill and much excitement I know,
Growing up I dared high and low.
The bungee jumps, parasails, deep water splash,
The roller coaster rides, climbs are always a bash.

Decades later, with two in tow these pearls,
I call them my heartbeats, my teenage girls.
What has changed, I am not sure,
I am more cautious as a mother can be here.

Brave and their forever rock I will be there,
Ready to fight the world without a care!
I may be safer now I know,
While my enthusiasm remains at the fore.

In this journey as a parent I have seen,
I am never perfect as it has been.
Every day as I teach them something new,
I learn with them about life and that is true.

Some days are just laughter, jokes and fun,
But as a mom, discipline is number one.
Books and social media try to define my role,
But I want to write my life scroll.

Being with them, every moment they need me,
Not forgetting my own timeout to set my mind free.
I am imperfect but not guilty you may see,
I am a human to feel that liberty.

Up in the clouds

Green grass, wooden deck, yellow swing, perched on
the 24th floor,
Almost touching the skies, in sync with my core.
The green may seem unreal to you,
But it's carefully put together by us two.

Every color, niche and decor you see,
Is our reflection with elegance and simplicity.
Family meals, the chatting teenagers in code,
Around the fireplace or in that private abode!

The evening coffee or prayer time rituals are there,
The weekly surprise meal is an experimental fare!
It's not an everyday feeling that one would know,
A cherished contentment of something hard to show!

Every corner of this house has something of me,
Every detail has a thought that I envisioned to see.
Battled with the experts on their rigid plan,
How will they define what is meant for my clan!

Today as I walk through every room, here I see,
Some beauty with several facets of our family.
My Mother lives next door so push it open,
An abode filled with warmth, is my safe haven.

After two decades of memories in our first nest,
Every learning there taught us to cherish the best.
A large community thrives here for sure,
Inviting and friendly, there is much cheer.

The calm is unthinkable with the city chaos here,
But we are nestled in a sanctuary peaceful and clear.
Am not sure what the future holds for us,
Definitely grateful to paint this poetic canvas!

With dreams and memories that we hope to cherish,
Several decades in this home is our wish.
Imperfections and chaos are mine to care,
Smitten with joy, this is my family's fare.

Did I dream for a different life here,
Not in this lifetime for sure!
Does my contentment lack ambition in your eyes,
I hold only my relationships in lows and highs.

Unlock

The many apps, my device has a universe of more,
Solving every problem or a small chore.
Staying connected is much wider than you can see,
It's no longer the phone conversation till eternity.

Sharing moments and pictures is quick for one,
Nothing is simple anymore, it could all be a pun.
Features are plenty, platforms are many too,
I might need a tutorial to survive in this tech zoo.

Smiling in a picture is not a norm today,
Covered faces pouts or filters are the way.
Chats are filled with slang, brevity and acronyms,
Paper letters have vanished from this hymn.

Faces are replaced in AI, homework is online,
More room for scams, plagiarism, yet all is fine.
A coffee catch up or a meeting at the office there,
Is now more often virtually quick to share.

The bank visit, savings or payments on time,
Is a forgotten memory with banking for every dime.
Gone are the days when wallets held coins and cash,
Heading out with a phone, just make the dash.

The grocery list that got us to the nearest store,
Limiting our task to the list or maybe one more.
Today every grocery is available on a click,
More than needed, reaching our doorsteps real quick.

Shopping in the crowded streets was fun,
Is now an online market for anything under the sun.
Film, plays, musicals so much in show,
The tickets are all here in tow.

Food, gifts, a small paper or key,
Send it anywhere through the delivery genie.
The gruesome visit to the doctor for an ache,
Is now an online consultation that we take.

Advice was an expertise of seniors, in our time,
Now a quick forward every group will always chime.
Books and pen, a student's might,
Now Google and virtual, only in sight.

Teachers taking classes in a room,
Videos are plenty, doubts are all cleared on zoom.
Cooking recipes handed down generations are lost,
Access global cuisines with videos at no cost.

A visual treat in theaters and televisions to cheer,
Is now on every phone with a plug in the ear.
Sitting at the table, conversations are missed,
Music, movies, memes, news are all pressed.

Shrilling victory in board games is much to cheer,
Family and friends it was simple for sure.
Every game has found a place on the screen,
Chess, Ludo, Pictionary, any game is seen.

Life has become easy, that's for sure,
But for lonely minds this is no cure.
Hold on to the days of hide and seek,
Don't let humanity feel so weak.

Paw-gratitude

Walking on four, following like no other,
An unconditional love that makes it tougher.
The eyes that love with such devotion,
As he looks at me with no condition.

He came to us, the size of my hand,
A true blessing, for many it's hard to understand.
No expectations, just shadows me everywhere,
Everything about him, I want to protect with care.

The family struggles to get his attention for sure,
The wave of a treat brings him much cheer.
Snuggle and belly rubs that's his anxiety cure,
Gazes with such intent unwavering and pure.

He is truly a baby in tow with me,
Carried in my arms or driving free.
Seated in front, his visual throne to watch sights,
Or snore through the honking in the traffic lights.

An animal lover, I might be,
But with this munchkin, it's a revelation to me.
Grateful and blessed to be chosen to be his person,
Hoping I am worthy of his reason.

We hope to be his family in every lifetime for sure,
Blessed to experience sheer joy with this miniature.
A novel learning every minute of the day,
A heartfelt life memory that is sure to stay.

4 AM

Before the sound of the alarm I hear,
The stillness in the wee hours of the morning here.
What began as a run for the body and mind,
Is now a morning ritual, leaving all behind.

A few stretches with some yoga too,
Every breath can be heard to be true.
Often I am asked about the joy of this 'me time',
Just with myself, it has an unbeatable rhyme.

As I make my way through the home in a hush,
I am followed by my fur baby in a rush.
Brewing that morning coffee tickles a chord,
The aroma and calm beats all odd.

Strange are the ways of the break of dawn,
The mind will not wander and will not be drawn.
How does the calm of the morning know my heart,
It has a different reset for a daily start.

Will I trade this time to stay snuggled in bed,
Even on a Sunday, nothing can be said.
It's a different version of 'me time' here,
After the early morning kitchen wrap there is cheer.

Most believe hobbies thrive the best before dawn,
So I string my words and ink the pages thereon.
This peace was broken with absolute scare,
I was shaken by a bandicoot at my door to care.

It had reached my grocery pile with ease,
But it was a fear like no other and not a tease.
Trembling to see how fearless it had been,
How did something so little appear so mean?

This visual stayed in my mind for several 4 am days,
 I chose to reset and add power in many ways.
While life dishes all shades of emotions to us I know,
I am grateful for the learning with which I grow.

2020- The year of uncertainty

A year that numbed and stayed on my mind,
Gripped with fear, I may not leave behind.
2020, a milestone for many, but a learning to me,
I turned 40, a new normal to see.

A virus they said, that shook the world,
Struggling with the unknown, inside we hurled.
An unseen monster is what it was called,
It was quick to spread and hard to be stalled.

To control the spread many have seen,
Lockdown mandates is what it had been.
Stay home, stay safe was a widespread plea,
It was a time for vitamins, immunity and hot tea.

With confusing symptoms treatments were unclear,
Home or hospital was a chance of fear.
The shortage of beds was definitely worrying,
For frontline folks, this battle was alarming.

Lime, turmeric, honey, spices and all,
Tips and tricks were plenty hoping to stall.
Hands washed, sanitized homes, we put our might,
We waged a war with the virus, it was our fight.

Vulnerable and risky is what they would say,
Above 60 and below 10 within homes should stay,
But the virus sees no gender, income, religion or age,
Illness and death, it was a common stage.

A sad time for many, time for tears,
Jobs were lost, business had shut in fears.
The economy hoped to come out, slow but strong,
Small steps were needed with no scope for wrong.

Digital and online redefined you and me,
Classes were online is what we could see.
Hiccups were many but learning was fun,
The kids missed all their time under the sun.

No longer did we stroll and walk away,
Missing our time soaking in the park on a sunny day.
The malls were empty, the customers were rare,
Home delivery was the best fare.

A gentle cough and sneeze to scare,
We no longer would bless instead we did glare.
The gym and pool were a tease to our fitness,
Fitness and chefs at home were the buzz to witness.

Our fashion mantra saw new sparks,
Though necessary, there was variety in masks.
Group Holidays and parties, a memory of yesterday,
Farewell handshake, hello Namaste!

Celebrations and meetings through a video call,
Business and communication had evolved for all.
The simple hug and pat were almost gone,
The eyes spoke, smiling masked, dusk and dawn.

We take nothing for granted, a lesson so true,
Our new normal; we are a new kind of crew.
A year we hope never comes back,
As we grapple with this normal with every hack.

Unmasked

The news was frenzy; it was a chatter of unknown,
The fear was looming and anxiety had grown.
Symptoms that confused, doctors were unclear,
Panic had struck many a tear.

Lockdown, masks, social distance they said,
Covid and its variations have much been read.
Masks have left the face of many for sure,
But it stayed as a wardrobe accessory here.

Covered or not it's no longer a shield of fear,
It's a human gap that's sadly very clear.
A generation went online and stayed hooked there,
From offline to online, now actual friends are rare.

When restrictions were lifted, crowds didn't care,
Losses were many, no one to spare.
A pandemic that made a lasting memory for sure,
Businesses and marriages were tested with no cheer.

Kids and pets born in this feared time,
Were protected in a bubble from the chaotic rhyme.
Too much noise or crowds created a worrying scare,
Counselled endlessly to make a balanced fare.

Four years later, reactions are mixed,
Some are still grappling with the fear that whipped.
While the new normal exists for some for sure,
Others have gone back to the carefree years.

While the adults are struggling to fight their fear,
The kids are grappling with mixed messages here.
Every generation sees a different view of life,
Parenting clashes are not free from strife.

Where did the innocence disappear today?
Dealt with a true reset, time to seize the day.
We hope it may be a thing of the past,
But with new views on life, make memories that last!

Zen - a true serenity

Sitting at the piano by the quaint street,
Transported by the music, from head to feet.
The traffic, chaos and noise I find,
Grips me with a vibe away from the daily grind.

I can feel the daunting steps I climbed that day,
The path that felt like it was heaven's way.
Many steep steps to the caves did I find,
Every step felt like a test of my mind.

Calming waters riding the bamboo boat,
Through the cave it was a happiness float.
Serene and peaceful it was a memory for sure,
Definitely in my mind bank so dear.

Surrounded by other boats and kayaks here,
Finding their way with much cheer.
The teasing monkeys on the rocky facade did smile,
Every nationality cheering loudly was a worthy mile.

Inside the cave, it was like nothing I had seen,
Every step seemed mysterious with a magical sheen.
Three chambers did we cross that day,
Nature's creation is spectacular in every way.

Every side in the cave had a formation so clear,
Figures were many, the echoes we could hear.
The cool touch of every side felt like a film,
Enraptured and jubilant up to the brim.

Standing up there it was the view of a lifetime,
Nothing seemed to matter worth every dime.
Sprawling water with boats under the rocky might,
If I was an artist I would paint this sight.

The decline had more sore for sure,
Our limbs would be unfelt to the core.
Every downhill I felt somber in my heart,
Leaving behind a sacred chant.

As we get ready to soak new sights,
This experience will stay for several days and nights.
For some it was an eventful itinerary in a trip,
For me it was a soulful emotion with a deep grip.

Soaring the skies

In the stillness of the night skies, high up here,
The flight wings glow in red, a view so clear.
The sky is decorated with stars so rare,
A painting in the sky etched with care.

The night seems long and so does the journey,
Restless minds are naturally in a hurry.
But small boosts make a memorable flight,
The weary mind is seeking a restful night.

The flight is steered by women with the reins they sit,
Such a treat to watch them take charge in the cockpit.
The rest of the crew were charming women too,
Makes an inspiring team far and few.

The dim lights in the plane soothe the guests to sleep,
Disturbed by the shrieking child's uncontrolled weep.
The tantrum of a toddler kicking the seat,
In this chaos, it's hard to get any sleep or eat.

As we eagerly wait to explore new sights,
With a schedule of our own, morning to night.
The pilot announced a plan to descend soon,
The sound that felt like a boon.

Through these hours, as we tried to find our calm,
The flight attendants tirelessly served with charm.
Uncomplaining they patiently answer every worry,
Without pushing back in a hurry.

Arrived and relieved to deplane here,
It's back home, or some new lands to explore.
Stories will be plenty, hopes are more,
Soaring the skies with much more in store.

Retirement abode

The sparkling golden waves, that lash before me,
Nature's miracle from my room I see.
The far horizon, I yearn to find the ocean end,
It's an endless and expansive legend.

Cuddled in my duvet, looking through the glass,
Blessed to see the sea from here not worth the pass.
The view was priceless and rare,
Touch of the ocean and the sand was my care.

The many surfers get there early to wave,
Waiting patiently for the best tide to brave.
Fitness enthusiasts run along the beach,
While others seek fitness in dance to teach.

Basking in the morning sun,
The radiance of this glory is no pun.
The calm that engulfs my mind with this sight,
Water is my therapy and hope is my might.

The orange aura that transcends to pink by sunset,
The colors are many, it's a confusing bet.
There are flowers blooming around with cheer,
It's a magical feeling to have all year.

By evening the beach gets busier for sure,
Adults and kids gather with much cheer.
The vibes of local food eateries and playful glee,
The lights sparkle the mood of every tree.

As I walked by the beach with much thought,
A soulful emotion that can never be bought.
How does the water calm with such ease,
The sea speaks to me without a tease.

Penchant for the sea when retirement knocks,
I don't yearn for mountains or a green habitat stock.
I do hope to find my solace here,
In deep slumber with the waves without fear.

War Cry

The room was full of people coiled in emotion,
Shaken to see, bursting their misplaced notion.
It was a reality no one could see,
It opened our eyes to a silent plea.

Every photo taken in the war,
Had a different turmoil from near and far.
Stories of anger, rage, deception and more,
Every chord of our being was hit to the core.

It wasn't just one war that they faced,
The agitation of decades that cannot be erased.
Countries were many, treaties were broken then,
Promises made were simply forgotten.

Hearts were broken as the harm didn't stop,
Generations were left with an irreparable scar.
While disability and mobility had impacted many,
Diseases and suffering left everyone edgy.

The brave soldier enters the battlefield with pride,
The enemy crossfire often is a dangerous ride.
The locals lose lives or with injuries get caught,
A shock to the routine of the day, no one had thought.

Like many countries, we have seen wars too,
My father braved a war here, for me and you.
His stories gripped conversations with my friends,
Who wished that the evening never ends!

Many countries have seen the bloodshed and tears,
Locals' mothers and children are gripped by fears.
The valour of so many gets lost in time,
Those who face it are scarred with a sad chime.

The commitment of a war journalist is shown,
Unbiased they present everything known.
Dodging bullets or missing the mines they tread,
An unfortunate miss and now it's a sorrowful read.

As we move along there thrives a generation here,
Who lives in a bubble of their own with much cheer.
Unaware of the turmoil of the heroes of our past,
It's imperative to give a showcase that will last.

Everyone has a battle of their own they fight,
Nothing is small or big in their right.
But as we look in our own way,
Never forget the larger country has much to say.

As we move ahead with our heads held high,
We hope conversations on unity have a macro cry.
The globe without disparity, as a whole we see,
With new strategies every country must referee.

Finding magic everywhere!

New places we go far and wide,
Every place has a mixed learning tide.
Some experiences just mark a niche in the mind,
So unique and memorable that it's hard to find.

I am a hippie tourist ready to photograph and pose,
A cheerful glee and my excitement shows.
Often disapproved of by my family for sure,
Capturing moments is my cheer.

Remarkable experiences across journeys were many,
Often thought worth every penny.
The cruise passing glaciers across the expansive sea,
Or the trek to caves to find my inner me.

The cheerful amusement parks give me a high,
Disney and other cartoons boost my wings to fly.
The walk on the calming beaches that lift my world,
Every second connected with the sea is gold.

The soft cool clinched fist of snow,
Ready to build the snowman with a plough.
The deep chord of the musical show,
An applause to every artist with a respected bow.

A grand dinner on a bus was such,
Savored with extravagance was a delightful touch.
Every dish bursts with flavor, taste and vibrance,
Tastefully decorated table that charmed the distance.

As we crossed the city's sights,
We were impressed with the sparkle of the lights.
Michelin star, the food was for sure,
An experience so rare, a comfortable bus tour.

Another calming experience we had,
By the river, a gastronomic experience, we were glad.
The surprising fountains erupted in front of us,
Swaying to the music and colored by light was a plus.

Grateful to have such glorious finds,
Around the world there is much to calm our minds.
I rather have a passport of every country to stamp,
Than a house full of things to make my life damp.

For many experiences I may fly far away,
The best remains in my balcony swing sway.
Sipping coffee with some precious family time,
Truly heartwarming in every rhyme.

Connected

Have you ever wondered about the time gone by,
A family we are born to, gives you wings to fly.
As we learn about the world around us,
Bitter or sweet, always around to cheer or fuss.

A perfectly imperfect family I have with me,
Ruffling through my fading memory from heaven
they see.
Struggling with choices and balance to find the calm,
Write our own story to protect us from harm.

Friends have no definition for sure,
School, college, work or home, in sadness and cheer.
Some equations walk the path for a lifetime of hope,
Silently anchoring our journey to cope.

Along the way as we go,
Some of our deepest bonds fail to show,
How did we hope that nothing will end,
Some friends like family don't find a way to mend.

Wise words will cure this broken heart,
Some bonds remain with us that far from the start.
Find your joy and learn for whatever time it may be,
Be grateful for the memories that set you free.

The forgotten friend or the distant cousin has shown,
Meaningful conversations in the unknown.
Sometimes the quick hi or the unknown help there,
Time can no longer define this care.

The innocent smile from a stranger,
Victim of habit, but a stranger is not always a danger.
A chord can be touched, in a second,
Give humanity a chance to be spiritually awakened.

The choicest brands, a larger life will not impress me,
Connected to the ground, reality is my key.
Relationships are placed on a pedestal so high,
Every effort to stay connected is my only try.

Decades later I am blessed with people to cheer,
Seasons changed, many emotions have transpired
here.
Today I seek solace in my now,
Rather than wasting time looking for how.

Life gets busy for you and me,
Steal a moment with your eternity.
A quick message, coffee or call,
Don't make excuses or try to stall.

Life is easy now for sure,
It's one click and you are connected here.
Social media defines every connection as your friend,
How do you check all is well offline at their end.

The smallest reaction to that big news,
Seeing the face to cheer for, is what I choose.
In this online universe of connected friends,
I choose my equations offline till my sanity ends.

We do not know what's in store for sure,
Living in the moment is our mantra here.
Seize the day and make it count now,
Live it right and take a bow.

Inspire and be inspired

Some words just stay in our hearts,
With much depth as a whole or in parts.
Words have always been a guide and friend,
Seeing life through inspiration till the very end.

Excerpts from The Paradox of Time defines it well,
It says bigger houses, smaller families to dwell.
Focus on more convenience but less time,
With emphasis on deep profits but shallow
relationships in the rhyme.

It further elaborates on more degrees, less sense,
With more knowledge, less judgment hence.
It explains how we reach the moon and come back,
But no time to meet the neighbour for a snack.

How accurately these words define this world now,
It's time to pause and make corrections somehow.
Don't we learn from experts they say,
Knowledge of the Dalai Lama is true in every way.

Another poem that speaks to my heart,
The words of Rudyard Kipling's 'If' play a big part.
It holds the character I aspire to be,
Hoping to be evolved amidst complex humanity.

Every word by Kipling, here he has shared,
A deeper meaning that I hope my children too cared!
To keep your calm and hold your head,
While not letting arrogance take over instead.

The poem dwells on loyalty and risks along the way,
Nurturing emotions and staying true night and day.
Life with integrity in any hardship it shows,
A balanced human is the way one grows.

As you soak in every facet he shares,
We see the value of time on earth having no spares.
The words will always echo in this lifetime for sure,
A strong guide and companion to cheer.

Another poet championing the world I recognise,
Maya Angelou whose words never seize to surprise.
'Phenomenal Woman' and 'Still I Rise' make me realise,
In small ways they are carved to revolutionise.

Her poems showcase struggle and fighting for more,
The never-give-up aura pushes to even the score.
While the struggles are different at every stage,
But perseverance is the hot button to engage.

I do hope you see the value of every icon of our time,
Every page you see, is a learning rhyme.
It's our duty to find the message here,
To leave an impact as footprints in the sands of time.

An ode to my lifelines

Holding you both in my arms many years ago,
The sentiments and joy, I can feel its echo.
With time you have moulded to perfection for sure,
It's hard to express my joy and cheer.

Now 16 & 13, two peas of the same pod,
Keepers of my heart, honest to God.
Every ounce of me, grips them tight,
Letting them go is my own fight.

Growing up we defined your way,
With values and life lessons within you to stay.
Now at this threshold of life, be a queen,
Paving your own path as much is to be seen.

You both are not young girls now,
To be told or explained the details on how.
You are not defined as women yet,
But with your wings to fly, you are set.

We will always hold you close,
Hope to save you from harm that could pose.
But any time you don't see us with you,
Find our strength within and that's your clue.

We are mighty proud of the person you both are,
Our kind of gems, a perfectly imperfect star.
Every lesson you learn on your own,
Build your character, be better in your zone.

Don't define your capability by others' script.
Be your own story, best to keep and worst be skipped.
An age so crazy that's for sure,
Friends will offer things, the mind may not be clear.

With every passing year, we cheer for you,
May every wish and success be yours so true.
Make your mistakes and learn much more,
Build life experiences and strengthen your core.

Be a leader, speak your mind,
Those innocent thoughts are hard to find.
Stay grounded, hold your own plea,
Win over humanity with peace and unity.

We are grateful to be chosen as your family too,
In every life I hope it's true.
May you always find a reason to smile,
Through this journey of life, mile by mile.

As I walk through life...

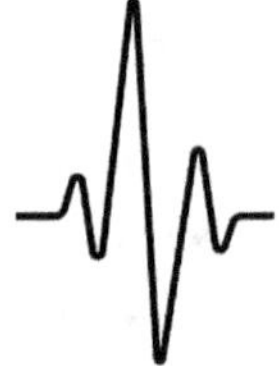

As I walk through life I see,
To act in an instant, happy and free.
Often impulsive and far from strife,
Consequences can be happy or a heartache for life.

As I walk through life I see,
A dream person, I hope to be.
Highs and lows the journey is a test,
It seems to take much longer to be the best.

As I walk through life I see,
Last spoken words may not set you free.
A sweet or kind word to a loved one you must share,
It may be the last time to show that you care.

As I walk through life I see,
Miles to go to set you struggle free.
Our own actions will penalise and hurt,
Making the impossible possible is a worthy effort.

As I walk through life I see,
Heroes come in shapes and sizes many,
To do what needs to be done at the right time,
In spite of the consequence, it's worth every dime.

As I walk through life I see,
The best moments with friends may not be easy.
Sometimes the ones you think might pull you down,
Will cheer you up with a reliable crown.

As I walk through life I see,
Maturity is not measured by the years you see.
Many birthdays come and go,
But the life experiences you had will truly show.

As I walk through life I see,
Looking back at memories with glee.
The wall credentials will applaud you with glory,
Be grounded, always find two sides to a story.

As I walk through life I see,
Families are weaved in the fabric of life till eternity.
Often some friends become families along the way,
Rare equations, you should be grateful in every way.

As I walk through life I see,
Tears and laughter have a true pact with humanity.
Memories are the lockstitch that weaves with care,
The tapestry of life with gratitude in a balanced share.

As I walk through life I see,
A journey so epic that it's worth every plea.
Much to do before I forever sleep,
Making every second count and blessings to keep.

The number game

The mind boggling syllabus, exhaustive and more,
The pressure is gripping, worrying to the core.
A little under 16, life decisions to be taken,
Careers chosen, decisions on subjects to be forsaken.

Burning the midnight oil, words complicate for sure,
Chapters are many, there is a looming fear.
The strong-minded courage up to face the war,
The planners find study hacks much before.

Many submissions, projects, assignments and more,
Topics may be dated but to be tested for sure.
Hours in a day seem to pass by quickly here,
Schedules are grappling, how do they clear.

The competition is gripping, it's definitely a worry,
Every small decimal percentage is grabbed in a hurry.
The future of the generation pegs on a number,
Talent, personality, character are in deep slumber.

Generations are tested with these markings here,
To produce a future in India or on the global shore.
Opportunities are plenty and much to choose here,
Bureaucracy makes it not so lucrative for sure.

The choice of stream, confused are most,
For the career counselor, the student is toast.
Science or commerce, taking the right step,
Humanities are a completely different mindset.

Admissions are nail-biting, an exam to test,
Previous transcripts and essays, it's another quest.
Deadlines to decide, fees to be paid,
No chance for a backup, plans must be laid.

Guidelines to the exam, it's a big puzzle to be seen,
With care and caution, students are keen.
The monitoring, corrections are such a serious point,
These are school kids, it's a forgotten viewpoint.

Exams are done, feeling liberated for sure,
Celebrations are planned, time to cheer!
Deep within, given your best,
The results are awaited for this big test.

Date for the results seems like a tease,
The news creates chaos leaving no one at ease.
The day is here, time to go online,
The doctrine of marks is detailed in every line.

A joyous moment for many for sure,
Many are disappointed with the missing marks here.
Curious about others marks on everyone's mind,
Hoping to be better, it's hard to leave behind.

A long way to go for education to evolve I know,
With different parameters we hope it's a better flow.
Just paused the pulsating stress with one,
An epiphany that the younger will face this sad pun.

Changemakers

In a world of my own, I am perplexed to find,
A life has been set, all fronts combined.
Often we ponder over the aches of the nation here,
Let's not just pass an opinion, swing to action gear.

Inspire and be inspired is what they say,
Fortunate to know heroes along the way.
In small ways I seek to learn every day,
With small acts of kindness I hope and pray.

At the Southernmost point of India we stood,
Bracing for India's on-foot journey she would.
With a hope to connect with women in every town,
Driving empowerment and safety without a frown.

A mission that was the vision of one,
But gathered global support, a reaction sure to stun.
With a voice in her head, she chose to be,
A true changemaker for generations to see.

Who says heroes are only with capes,
It's not Marvel or Batman changing shapes.
People around us have an unseen cape for sure,
Spot the hero and boost the champion cheer.

Champions of causes are the ones that rise,
One step at a time, success is no surprise.
Find that hero within you,
Change is from within and that's so true.
You can be the one that sits on the sides,
Hoping someone will take the initiative in this ride.
Be a part of the solution to the problems here,
Rather than being the problem and living in fear.

More often issues seem large and complex to ease,
Don't let the pessimists be a tease.
Put your mind to a cause that has your heart,
With passion and commitment, it's a quick start.

Water from air, electricity from the sun,
Many finds, there is a big invention that will stun.
Engaged campaigns, collaborate and join to care,
So many ways to help it's an easy share.

Weather, women, children, health and animal joy,
Funds, helping hands or time you can employ.
If nothing is promising, find a simple way,
A mission-driven run is an easy play.

The world is changed by your example, they say,
Not by your opinion, so act today.
Age is not a factor to power change, we must remind,
The famous words, *'One small step for man, one giant leap for mankind.'*

The Colour Palette

The torrid rains, washing away the dust,
Gather shade, everyone must.
A suddenly hot sunny day has changed now,
Feels like a different season somehow.

Blue skies turned gray,
The green trees with mighty winds sway.
Water flooding on the roads we see,
Traffic is mayhem, the road home feels like eternity.

The cleared rains, the canvas has changed now,
A stunning rainbow, it's a painting worth a wow.
Every color radiates with hope,
Take your pick, many colors in this rope.

A vivid blue purple, the deep violet they say,
Wisteria Blooms or Orchids, seize your charm today.
Spiritual and creative will be your tool of choice,
Empathetic and thoughtful, all in this poise.

Visualise the indigo night sky sparkle those stars,
Indulge blueberries and soak the healthy powers.
The brush with tranquility and mystery has this hue,
Dreams can be many and they do come true.

Is it the blue of the skies that lure,
Or does the calm of blue waters rest your fear.
Does it give you the freedom and imagination,
It also epitomises depth, sincerity and inspiration.

Soak in the green of nature in every tree,
Rather than turning green in jealousy and envy.
Refreshing and tranquil is what it says,
Cherish the abundance in the best ways.

Radiate and shine like the yellow in the sun,
Or bloom in glory like the sunflower has begun.
The aura has a magic that transpires everyone,
The optimism and energy, a worthwhile run.

The juicy orange or the papaya has much to add,
The glory of the patriotic saffron in the flag is no fad.
There is freshness, excitement and warmth in this,
The playfulness is much deeper for any of us.

The bright strawberry or the stunning red rose,
Choose wisely as red blood with anger glows.
The color of the heart, can rage at times,
But the passion and warmth can sing other rhymes.

Every shade of the rainbow has a palette that shows,
So many auras that the world knows.
But black and white has a niche of its own,
Stark opposites but each a beauty in their zone.

Find yourself in the white of salt or playful snow,
The graceful swan or a pearl teasing to show.
Soak in this purity with new beginnings from here,
A clean slate, there is so much to cheer.

Blink those black eyes, flaunt the hair,
Avoid old tales with the evil eye or black cat fare.
Elegance, classic and a glamour that glows,
The black diamond attracts a rare energy that flows.

Many colors, one soul for you and me,
Adorn them all, in different streaks and see.
Create a rainbow with a world that celebrates you,
Your life canvas will be unique and true.

The City Vibe

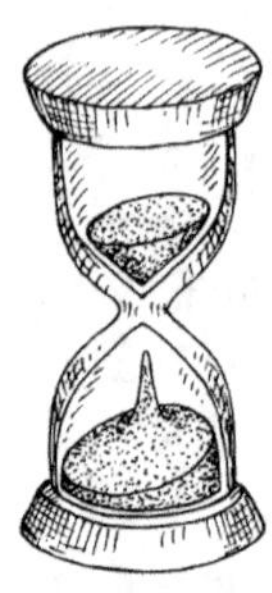

Walking the streets, the humidity was much,
Bustling crowds, pacing fast as such.
Work to be done, time is the essence here,
Diligent and focused much to steer.

With a dream to make it big they come,
Sacrifice and struggle is the journey hum.
Balance with work and small ways to relax today,
The spirit is something else night and day.

Small homes at a big price,
Unreachable for many, high in the skies.
The skyscraping skyline on the posh road,
A stark contrast to the slums, a struggle that showed.

The many cars that make their way,
While others seek solace in the trains everyday.
Every street has food joints and cuisines here,
The choices are many for the glasses to cheer.

The screaming hawkers, the mounting clothes stalls,
The first sight of the street markets will appall.
Finding the right product in the melee here,
Winning the perfect bargain is the reward for sure.

For a cooler time to shop, there is more to pay,
The malls are there every day.
But nothing like that chaos and the big steal,
Bags in tow, feels like a cracked deal.

A long day at work, yet ready to unwind,
A walk in the park or the beach to clear the mind.
Weekends are here, a play or show to see,
At dusk, dressed up to party with glee.

A historical showcase with edifices now far and few,
The city has character, where old meets new.
Breathing its own life, with a language of dreams,
With a rhythm of its own, there are many themes.

Every inhabitant has a different story to tell,
Pushing boundaries, defying odds well.
The working class labourers try to make ends meet,
It's a struggle for most and no easy feat.

Students burn the midnight oil,
With aspirations many, careers cannot foil.
Artists create masterpieces that show their zest,
Entrepreneurs are taking risks and hope for the best.

Each is a stranger in this universe here,
Ease of sharing stories, struggles with each other.
No longer are they unknown and alone,
United in this unyielding struggle to ace the zone.

The city will see floods, attacks or looming fear,
The spirit of the people, that finds the cheer.
There is no time to pause or deliberate there,
With resilience, they move forward with care.

This city teaches about hope,
The collective spirit and perseverance to cope.
The deep gratitude echoes a shared belief we know,
The liberal and accepting minds that go with the flow.

My home and heart are set with other towns for sure,
But the spirit of that city will always inspire me here.
I may not thrive in the same pace that exists there,
But with gratitude and perseverance, much to share.

The Celebrity Awe

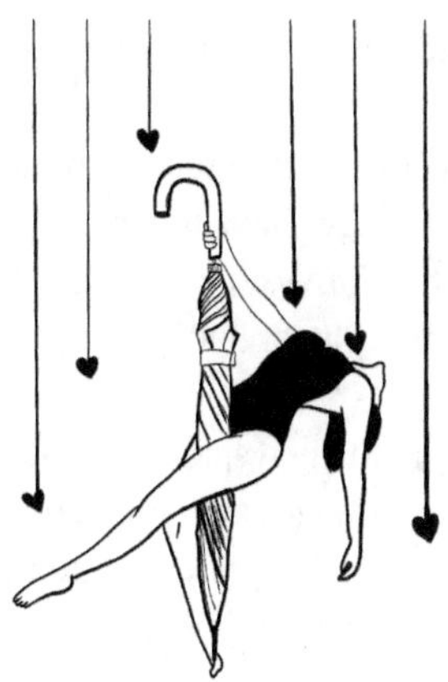

First day first show is all we hear,
The excitement and thrill is loud and clear.
The television, newspapers, internet, have this frame,
Everyone is chanting the same film name.

Is it the cast or the storyline that made the news,
Language can be any, subtitles are the cues.
The film thrives or flops, hard to say,
But the celebrity is now an icon to stay.

Walking the streets, much to be done,
Often there is a celebrity spotted in the sun.
Some make it more dramatic than others for sure,
The guards and trailing contingent, a spectacle here.

The cameras click rapidly in all the chaos here,
The crowd is eagerly pushing their might with cheer.
A small glimpse, or that selfie memory they hope,
With that celebrity in awe they cope.

Their homes are a spot to tour in awe,
Their lives no longer have the privacy law.
The spotlight and invasion feel unsettling to most,
A helpless cry, a platter hard to boast.

The columns in the newspapers track them close,
The social media pages are a bigger dose.
The many Paparazzi capture the little details here,
At any location, every glimpse is dear.

The celebrity families have lived this drama in life,
It's the toddler and not just the parents, or wife.
While this glory seems to be a thrill for most,
It seems like a dilemma and a nightmare to coast.

For most it's that classic fan moment there,
Where every effort seems worthy to care.
Definitely a celebrated virtuoso to get this cheer,
But is it worthy of the larger-than-life aura here?

For most the lines seem blur,
Public and private, it's a mystery to steer.
While the job seems to have its own stress for sure,
This unseen public pressure is definitely no cheer.

Beyond the Celebration - Marriage

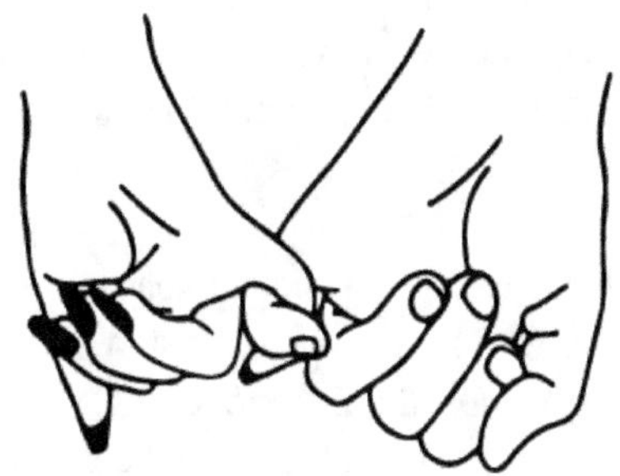

Blessings, flowers, tradition and fun,
Say cheers, come on everyone,
A bond to cheer and treasure for life,
Hurrah, Hurrah, it's time to be man & wife!

Traditionally arranged or love marriage it can be,
Both are tricky with much to learn and see.
The wedding day feels like a dream,
But living together will be a different scheme.

There is beauty, love and charm,
This companionship can be your calm,
Trust, love, joy and dependability,
Be each other's pillar till infinity,

It's definitely not a bed of roses,
Neither is it just romantic holidays and poses.
The challenge is real and so is the heartbreak,
The compromise and adjustment have much at stake.

The balance is an adventure of its own,
Extended families and relatives, it's a confusing zone.
But every equation won over with love and care,
Will reward a lifetime of emotional wealth, forever
rare.

Some fights may keep each other apart,
And wonder who should make the start,
Stash the ego, make the first move,
A simple apology and both back in the groove.

We love our freedom; we love our free heart,
But draw a line, right from the start,
Share those dreams, make memorable days,
Family before self is the mantra always.

Life gets busy as time flies away,
Cherish moments and recreate magic every day,
Share the light, watch the stars,
Simple hand holding and believe in magic powers.

Who am I?

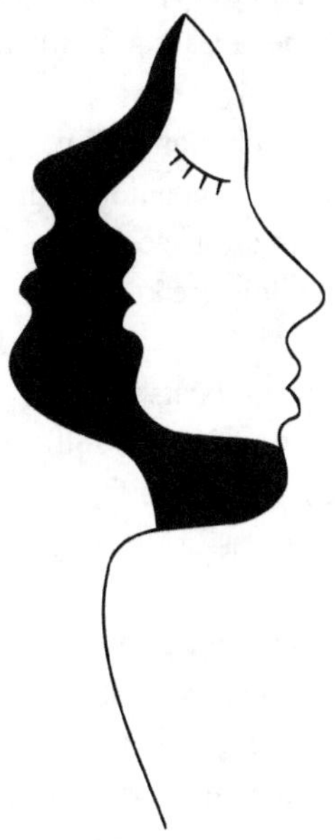

The little girl has grown to be,
I am a daughter is what you see.
Shaped in ways that they hoped I become,
Still learning in this role, a long way I have come.

Almost like twins, a sister to him,
Every milestone was the perfect hymn.
Keeper of secrets, the best I have seen,
Was an anchor through my journey as a teen!

Nurtured and loved with stories that shaped,
As a granddaughter to a magic world I often escaped.
An equation that had a short time frame,
But carried with me, a lasting family name!

Life gifted me an anchor and calm,
I became a wife and companion to my prince charm.
A new phase of life did I see,
Balance was definitely the key.

Blessed with two heartbeats for sure,
Motherhood teaches you to be selfless with cheer.
Shaping two teens, as I learn from my mistakes too,
Many emotions here as I ride this journey through.

Walking on four but loving beyond any I know,
This fur baby has so much to show.
To love unconditionally is what I have seen,
Unlike any other, the purest it has been.

Over the years, made friends that matter,
Holding me close when life was about to shatter.
No judgements or expectations that pull me down,
These are the wings that will never let me drown.

Every equation has something that gives me hope,
But they do not define me, they help me cope.
I have a voice, values and beliefs that are mine,
Steering my own journey, I am my own spine.

An identity is what everyone hopes to make,
Careers and home, a balance that must not shake!
While building a life, falling behind some pace,
It's my unique journey; I am not part of the race.

The mind often battles with mindsets that clash,
My heart has no motivation with the material dash.
Small joys and memories make the heart smile,
Disconnected from many, but it's a worthy mile.

Life mantra

Every day we learn something new
We cherish and believe it all to be true.
We have learnt to live with hope and cheer,
To be able to view life happily without fear!

As time goes by, looking back as it was,
It's time to reflect with gratitude and a pause!
We have laughed and cried,
There will always be memories that can't be denied.

It's been a mixed bag but we will ride,
With hope and love we will cross this tide.
We had time to introspect and heal,
Connected and shared that's how we feel.

We cheered milestones in joy,
We learnt lessons in every ploy.
We have faults and mistakes,
A little change is all it takes.

We cared enough to cry,
We feared enough to protect and try.
We believe in life, reality and hope,
We know tomorrow is our real scope.

We cherish this life with us,
That gave us the strength to see the plus.
Wishing you love, cheer and the best,
With loved ones through any test.

We have aspirations, but we dote on contentment,
Making memories, humbled at every achievement.
Build equations not defined by frequency or reason,
Thrive on the bond to last every season.

We all have losses deep in the heart,
Acceptance and optimism is the key from the start.
Conversations will differ, from 'is' to 'was',
Past for the world, present in our hearts is the pause.

Philosophies and beliefs will always be the key,
That is the way life should be.
Optimism is the guardian angel, reality is a friend,
Mistakes in every role, but no regrets till the end.

May there always be humility and calm,
Stay grounded and away from harm.
A blessed lifetime is what we pray,
Be fabulous, be you, is all we say.

Shadow along

As I walked up the dark street,
The roads had dim lights every few feet.
It was a lonely stretch with buildings lined there,
The sound of my footsteps echoed in the square.

In the still night, I felt a presence behind,
It felt like kindred spirits were on my mind.
The void by their absence was felt so much,
Wondered if it was a presence or chance of their
touch!

Hopeful to have that departed dear one pace with me,
To fulfill the incomplete conversations with glee.
It felt as if more memories were yet to be made,
My heart was not ready for the equation to fade.

With no one else around to be seen,
While hoping for these spirits seem gleam.
There was a fear of the unknown force,
It was time to see the source.

I gently looked over my shoulder to catch a sight,
Finding no one I did feel light.
I did miss the possible hope there,
Then I found my shadow following me with care.

This dark figure silently moved with me,
Unspoken words but matching steps till eternity.
The endless journey without complaining here,
Even in darkness so much to learn from my rear.

There is truly so much uncertainty that thrives,
But the darkness of the shadow felt alive.
For the thinker it doesn't want to be seen there,
For the believer it's never to be alone silently to care.

It's all about perspective for you and me,
We have our own views of life till eternity.
Every light must have a shadow they say,
Hang in there; you have a companion forever to stay.

Young at heart

Years of experience is what they say,
Many stories in this lifetime from black to grey!
Learnings are many that's for sure,
With patience and joy they share with cheer.

Every year of their life has shaped homes with care,
Raising humans with values, integrity and flare!
A prayer of gratitude for every guidance we get,
Inch by inch we are moulded as a perfect set.

Things may not be found, because it's kept so safe,
Need not worry; it's probably not worth the chafe.
With peace they hope to hear,
There may be a struggle, but sense of love for sure.

The grey hair and the wrinkles of the skin,
Not a pattern in everyone, some age like gin.
The mind and body has much might in some,
An inspiration to many, for generations to come.

The mind sometimes might forget a name,
Efforts to sharpen in Sudoku or a number game.
Emotion and a soft heart can be a worry,
Sometimes confused, what might offend in a hurry.

The pace has slowed but the heart keeps speed,
The mind is active and has much to heed.
The eyes have doubled from two to four,
Fancy frames are on, never miss a chore.

Hands on, with every area that might seem,
Wanting to be independent that's the only dream.
House chores and utility demands are there,
Steer the wheel, time to socialise and share.

A generation that has evolved with new fads,
Decades offline, now dabble with mobiles and iPads.
The journey from offline to online needed some time,
But learning was quick, shopping is worth the dime.

Competing or not, they don't like the term old,
Every story may repeat, but it feels like gold!
Young at heart in every area you will find,
But availing the senior benefits they will not mind.

A retired life, is what they have for some,
Travel the world, much is yet to come.
The talented hobbyists or the green finger champs,
Create beauty with the simplest stamps.

The generation pegs on conversations and time,
Doting on grandchildren is another rhyme.
Teenagers find it hard to connect to care,
The chats are changing, it's a brief fare.

Parenting has changed and so have the ways of life,
Debates can be endless but are not worth the strife.
Opinions differ, they often hope for their own clone,
Often forgetting, their little one has grown with a
mind of their own.

Age is just a number is what they say,
But surely they are the life of any party everyday,
Lived life on a philosophy of their own,
With grace and charm, they have grown.

As my days number, I often ponder and find,
In my early 40's but can be further behind.
I have much to learn from the silver surfers here,
A life charter, on how to age with cheer.

I promise

Promises are many, hard to keep,
Often to be reminded, much too deep!
I promise to be a better version of myself every day,
An effort for sure, but that's what I pray.

I promise to see a point of view that is not my own,
Learn something new and not be blown.
I promise to be true to my heart,
Cherishing moments from the very start!

I promise to be able to speak my mind,
Than hoping others will seek my worries and find.
I promise to be open and inspired,
While striving to inspire and be rightly admired.

I promise to find it in my heart to forgive and forget,
Letting go may be a challenge, but I must let.
I promise to admit I may be wrong along the way,
Make amends and learn before the end of the day.

I promise to not judge your past or present choices,
Respecting them, in spite of the surrounding noises!
I promise to see you as your own person,
Not trying to mould you into my vision for certain.

I promise that life cannot be taken for granted I know,
Moving slowly with gratitude and a mind to grow!
I promise that there will be mistakes I will make,
Be patient, I will correct them, so don't forsake.

I promise to be the keeper of hearts,
Guarding relationships that thrive in our life charts!
I promise people change and we must accept,
Know that every promise must be honored and kept.

Coffee

Sipping coffee, sitting on my swing,
It's the calm of a new day, my happy ring.
Many reports, contradict its worth to health,
But one cup for me is the greatest wealth.

Marching down memory lane with mom on a day
Coffee in hand, makes it a perfect way.
Every evening, with my husband has a deep tone,
Of comfort and gratitude, with patience I hone.

Friends like family, check in now and then,
Catch up over coffee is a perfect ten.
The forgotten conversations with an old friend,
Hope that time stands still, the cup must not end.

As a person that calms with the sea,
The green flora is not my cup of tea.
But my roots have strong coffee vibes,
Ingrained in the coffee plantation are my tribes.

The sight of the blossoms is a real treat,
Lush green and white, it's a different beat.
Every plant has so much to share,
Generations have reaped them with much care.

The rainfall, manure, price, labour is the daily buzz,
Any other topic and there is no fuzz.
Social obligations are the breaks from the grind,
For the onlooker, it's a strange unwind.

Acres of land sprawling with coffee plants,
Treading with care, avoiding wildlife chants.
Mankind and wildlife, coexist or not,
A menace and danger, try to be the planter escort.

The scenery is magical, I cannot deny,
The stillness grips in ways that's worth a try.
Every generation has a duty to care for the land,
Plant by plant, bearers of flora so grand.

The day begins with the rising of the sun,
The planter rushes and dogs circle the plantation run.
We are holding this land with pride,
But what's the future with the next generation to tide.

The alarm shrills, not one but two,
Annoyed with the sound, they snooze, this lazy crew.
Their human alarm, must appear with the shriek,
Imagine the sacred coffee is in their hands to seek.

Every generation has something new that sticks,
It may be radical, who knows what grips.
Whatever path they choose for their own,
With a coffee in hand, they will tread the unknown.

Finding Equanimity

Equanimity is a sublime emotion for some,
Neutral and aloof one may become.
But I see the warmth and glow that thrives,
A state of being that everyone strives.

Equanimity gives a different sense of peace,
Undisturbed and serene, unlocks life keys.
Often seen with patience for sure,
There is no unwanted reaction or pressure.

Being driven by an inner calm,
Mindfulness and balance allow no harm.
Surely equanimity is a life learning I see,
In every direction, I strive till eternity.

Hoping for praises, quick to blame,
Success or failure it's a tricky game.
Fame and pain see the same end,
Attachment unfortunately has no mend.

Am I ready to find this equanimity in life,
Thriving on deep emotion it's definitely a strife.
Having the same emotion towards everything I hear,
Is a challenge and a long way to go for sure.

While emotions can be tricky I know,
Build your character instead of material to show.
Make memories of a life that is short,
Who has seen tomorrow, today is all I have got.

An excess of anything is harmful they say,
Choosing people who give this aura is a hard play.
Striking the balance, keep distractions at bay,
The journey is a challenge, I must practice everyday.

Life experiences can be many,
Unreactive and calm, worth every penny.
Letting go is the best mantra for sure,
Live, love and laugh, there is so much to cheer.

I am no sage, nor intend to be one,
Life is in color and that's no pun.
Striving for equanimity may be the hope,
But along the way in little emotions I will cope.